"For the person who balks at tests, struggles, and hardships, this book will challenge them to see life through a more positive lens. Author, preacher, teacher, and scholar Rev. Catherine Griggs offer us all a prescription for healing and assuaging any adverse responses to pressure. Borne from the bowels of personal experiences, "A Diamond in the Rough" is a mandate for enduring life's journeys over rocky terrain until irrevocable brilliance illumines our path and becomes our destination."

Reverend Phyllis T. Hilliard
Cathedral International, Perth Amboy, NJ

"Diamonds go thru a process to become the beautiful stone that is adored by many in the world today. In this book, "A Diamond in the Rough" the Lord has commissioned Catherine Griggs to help you find the diamond within you. Though the process isn't enjoyable now, the Scripture declares, "Weeping may endure for a night, but joy comes in the morning." Allow this book to aide you thru the process as you discover your hidden treasure."

Pastor Ishmael Wilson, Senior Pastor
Another Level Church, Capitol Heights, MD

"For anyone who has ever asked the question, "Why me?" or "Why is this happening to me?" God has heard and answered in "A Diamond in the Rough." This book is inspiring, biblically based, enlightening and a must read!"

Eunice Timley, Assistant Pastor
The New Hope Baptist Church, Newark, NJ
Author of *Praises of Warfare*

A Diamond In The ROUGH

Discovering The Brilliance In You

Catherine A. Griggs

Diligence Publishing Company
Bloomfield, New Jersey

The Scripture in this book is from various versions of the Bible including, but not limited to the King James Version and the New International Version. Some Scripture is also paraphrased and put in the author's own words.

A DIAMOND IN THE ROUGH

Copyright © 2014
Diligence Publishing Company
P.O. Box 2476, Bloomfield, New Jersey

Front Cover Design by: Melissa Rivers

All Rights Reserved

No part of this book may be reproduced in any form without the written permission from the publisher except for brief passages included in a review.

To contact Rev. Catherine Griggs for bookings to preach or speak at your church, organization, send email to:
diamond.ministries@yahoo.com

A DIAMOND IN THE ROUGH

ISBN: 978-0-9727416-6-8

Printed in the United States

Table of Contents

Dedication

Acknowledgements

Foreword

Introduction

Chapter One: *No Pressure No Diamond*..................23

Chapter Two: *In The Process Of Time*......................39

Chapter Three: *Perseverance: Fighting For Your Future*..............................61

Chapter Four: *Polished To Perfection*......................79

Chapter Five: *Fulfilling Your Purpose: Letting Your Brilliance Shine*..................89

About The Author

Order Information

Dedication

I dedicate this book to the greater glory and honor of the Father, the Son and the blessed Holy Spirit. Who without Your prompting, leading and guiding, none of the words in this book would be possible. You continue to reveal in me Your brilliance, and You encourage me daily to rely on Your grace, which is all sufficient! I thank You for unceasingly empowering me to shine bright like a diamond, and share the Word of God with the people of God, that I may encourage, edify and challenge people to live victorious Christian lives!

A Diamond in the Rough is also dedicated to my greatest joys and blessings in my life (outside of my sons), my granddaughters, JaHara and Laila. As the song goes, "I Never Knew Love Like This Before!" You two inspire Glam Ma to let my light shine more brightly, and to avail myself more to the plans that the Lord has for my life! I declare and decree that both of you will be powerfully, anointed and appointed women of God that will shine brightly and fulfill the call of Christ on your lives. May the Holy Spirit always reign in your lives, and may the power of Christ *overshadow your every step. Truly, eyes have not seen, ears have not heard, neither has it entered into the heart of man the good things that the Lord has in store for the two of you! (1 Corinthians 2:9)*

Lastly, I dedicate this book to Steven D. Brown, who was the only survivor in a car accident that killed his cousin and his best friend in 2010. Steven, I told you on Good Friday 2014, that GOD's plans for why He spared your life would soon be revealed, as you shared with me how you were struggling on that day, the anniversary of the accident. The Lord's resurrection power and brilliance is housed within you. I pray that this book helps to release you into the greater work that God has for you. Let your light so shine, Steven, that you may bring glory to GOD and thereby, discover the meaning for your life!!!

Foreword

It has been my privilege to serve as the Senior Pastor for The Reverend Catherine Griggs for over 15 years.

During that time, I have watched her grow, work, study, raise a family, and be a wife, all full-time. And through it all, I have seen her endure hardship as a good soldier; and yet, find the strength to throw up her hands and praise! Hers is a life of praise, prayer, and commitment.

A faithful wife, mother, and daughter, she indeed is an example of one who knows that "where there is no pain, there is no gain!"

In addition, she serves as the Superintendent of the Sunday School Department of a mega church; with one Church in three locations. And is also a very capable Senior Executive Assistant to the Senior Pastor and CEO; which is not an easy job.

In her first publication, *A Diamond in the Rough,* she speaks about how the power of pressure is designed to make us, and not to destroy us. For in the process of time, if we will persevere, God indeed will polish us to perfection, and our purposes will be fulfilled. I encourage this read to all! Particularly in this hour where there seems to be a challenge on every side of the globe and nation, we need to press beyond life's pressure situations.

Congratulations daughter! The best is yet to come!

Bishop Donald Hilliard, Jr., D. Min.
Lead Pastor, Cathedral International,
Perth Amboy New Jersey

Foreword

It is not very often that the instructor has an opportunity to observe from an objective perspective the progress of their student. In many instances, we are hubris as we seek ways to pride ourselves on the accomplishments that those who have been assigned to us have achieved, negating their hard work and struggle.

I am so grateful for the journey of this author, who I have known more than twenty years, and to share this heartfelt expression of her growth and development. The evidence exhibited through her transparency and chronicled details of *"A Diamond In The Rough"* is refreshing, inspiring, and outright riveting!!!!

Enjoy the contents of these pages; then perhaps you will get a glimpse of the exhilaration, knowing that when you plant seeds in fertile ground, you will experience as I have, the joy of the harvest!!!!!!

Still in one peace

Pastor Lula A. Baker
Cross and Crown Christian Church,
South Orange, New Jersey

Acknowledgements

Over the past decade, there have been numerous people that have encouraged me, prayed for me, and reminded me that *A Diamond in the Rough* needed to be written.

First and foremost, I give God thanks for my fun, quirky, and anointed family. To my husband John, (Poo-moonie): Thank you for always believing in me and the gifts that God has entrusted to me. You have been the greatest cheerleader (oops, I meant spiritual trainer) that has prompted me on to complete this work. Your words were life to me, and helped me in times of stagnation to believe that I would complete this book. Thank you!

To my strongest critics, but most honest and sincere sons, J.D. and Malcolm: Divinely orchestrated, you both would say inspirational and deep thoughts that would prompt me to write and were so aligned with the book, that only in the mind of GOD could they be formed. Thank you always for truly affirming and confirming for me that my greatest title to date is that of Mother. I am blessed to be yours!

To Rocky, our Pit Bull/Terrier: I thank GOD for allowing you to enter the life and hearts of our family. Playing with you helps to ground me and refocus me at times; and you truly are a Griggs at heart.

In memory of my dad, Lee Grande Smith, whose habitation is with our Father in heaven, thank you for loving me unconditionally, and for being a great example of a kind, thoughtful provider and father.

To my mom, Carrie King, you have always been my greatest mentor and supporter, and I thank God for your unyielding belief in me, and your nuggets of wisdom along the way that always let me know that nothing is impossible to them that believe! Your strength and grace in the face of your greatest challenge is phenomenal. And that's you, a phenomenal woman!

To my one and only sibling, Concetta; as an author and pastor, you have shown me that our words can be memorialized and shared with the world, and that our stories and experiences can transcend time and space and help others. What a wonderful example. To my brother-in-law, June, and my nephews, Derek and Denzel: thank you for your love and support over the years. I cherish you.

To my great-nephew Ayden, thank you for bringing more love, joy and laughter into our lives. To my mother-in-law Irene Griggs, my father-in-law, Monroe Pair, and to my cousins Cindy and MaKayla, thanks for the times of family fellowship, always coupled with laughter. You guys are fun to be with, and I love you.

To my inner circle friends, Dawn Rivers, Tina Adams, Brenda Woods, Durelle McPherson, Margie Barbee, Sheila Campbell-Haugabrook Stephanie Bush, Renee Sims and Rebecca Simmons: Your friendship means the world to me. Thank you for the laughter and the tears; thank you for the prayers and the pushing; thank you for the trust and the teaching; and thank you most importantly for being a safe-space and exemplifying what TRUE inner circle friendship means; Love, trust and dependability!

To Bishop Donald Hilliard, Jr., Pastor Bernadette Glover (Cathedral International), and Pastor Lula Baker (formerly of New Hope Baptist Church, now of Cross and Crown Christian Church), thank you so much for being the divinely chosen spiritual mentors that GOD selected at specific and distinct times in my life. GOD used you to motivate me to stretch and move me out of my comfort zone, while also helping me to mature me in the ways of God, and to train me in ministry. As my spiritual coverings, you reprimanded me when I would shrink back in fear and doubt, while also loving me and praying for me through difficult seasons.

Thank you for loving me and believing in me enough to take on the challenge (and a challenge I was and still am at times), but also for not crushing my soul during the times when I just could not or would not go higher! Bishop Hilliard, your work ethic is unparalleled; Pastor Glover, your love for GOD and His righteousness is remarkable; Pastor Baker, your passion for GOD and GOD's people is infectious! Thank you for your example. The three of you always made me feel like I mattered to you, and ultimately you displayed to me in unconscious ways that I mattered to GOD!

Special thank you's to Sheronia Rogers, Judy Green, Renee White, Hope DuBois, Geraldine Delaney and Valerie Jacobs for being a strong group of anointed women and friends that have provided great encouragement throughout the years. Your words of wisdom, prayers and support have been invaluable.

Finally, Jeff "Tariq" Cooper, I have never forgotten your words of encouragement during these past 10 years. You were one of the first people to encourage me to write this book, and even gave me a shout out at a cookout in 2004 publicizing *A Diamond In the Rough*, and encouraging people to buy it when released. Let me just say, better late than never…Lol!

Introduction

I began writing *A Diamond in the Rough* over 10 years ago, and yet it could not be released until this year because this is the year that I really began to understand at a deeper, deeper level the significance of GOD's divine grace in my life. "5" is the number for grace, and GOD showed me how He has given me a double portion of grace ("10") to be able to not only finish this book, but to also see its place in His divine order of things.

GOD spoke to me very clearly in 2012 and told me that He would be downloading what He wanted to be released on the earth to those who had an ear to hear in a greater way through songs, movies, and books. In a way, we would be modern day scribes dictating His premier thoughts, words and topics that would be released at a certain time in the earth. *A Diamond In The Rough* is such a work, and the premise of the book is an idea, a metaphor that GOD wants released in this hour!

At the inception of writing this book, GOD began to show me the similarities between the complex process that a diamond undergoes in its creation, and the extremely detailed and layered formation of a servant leader in Christ. Both diamonds and Christians endure a very rigorous process that seems on one hand to be aggressive and counter-productive, but ultimately, actually *"works together for good"* and for purpose!

Diamonds are rare gems that are made under immense pressure and are birthed in the depth's (or core) of the earth's surface in obscurity. Hidden from the naked eye, diamonds endure a rigorous process in their formation and thus are considered very valuable due to the great investment of time and supernatural occurrences that bring forth their brilliant manifestation. Once revealed, diamonds are unique in their make-up, and no two diamonds are identical as they each have their own particular "characteristics" that make them one of a kind!

The word "diamond" in the Greek is "Adama," which means "indestructible." As the strongest of all precious gemstones, diamonds can survive any force or pressure placed upon them. They have the highest "critical stress intensity factor," which is the amount of pressure a gem can be squeezed under before altering its shape. The diamond's "toughness," which is its ability to withstand forceful impact, also far exceeds all other gemstones. Thus, a diamond can withstand great amounts of pressure and force, far more than any other gemstone, and still emerge as an exquisite and expensive treasure! Ten years ago, GOD gave me the revelation of how diamonds and His chosen vessels are formed in a similar manner!

The process that we as Christians endure in obscurity that works to shape our character and develop us into mature servants of GOD appears to share related elements. Comparable to the diamond, children of GOD seem to experience periods of great testing and pressure; we learn to develop mental and emotional toughness through our trials and afflictions; we find ourselves in heated situations that bring out our *charater*-istics; and prayerfully, after years of submission to GOD and the process, we finally emerge as vessels of honor whose value is priceless and anointing is costly! Like the diamond, we are able to tolerate forceful impacts and large amounts of stress that work to build our character without breaking us or rendering us useless or devalued. As called out believers, we have our own "critical stress intensity factor" and level of "toughness" that allows us to bend without breaking!

Every diamond is unique and has distinct markings and cuts in it that render each gem a Designer's original. Similarly, GOD has fearfully and wonderfully created each and every one of us! None of us share the same fingerprints or the exact same genetic make-up. We are each uniquely fashioned. And yet, with all of this divine creativity as humans that are formed by the Master's design, unfortunately, some of us do not discover the revelation of our own self-worth for many years or decades…. Sadly, some of us live hampered and hindered by demonically calculated abuses, disappointments and afflictions, oftentimes living as "diamonds in the rough" with our own brilliance hidden from us until we are awakened through: **great Pressure; a prolonged Process; fiery trials that teach us how to Persevere, and Polishing that smoothes out our rough edges**. Once awakened, we are able to be positioned for GOD's purpose for which we were created! Previously obstructed but not destructed, we undoubtedly break free from the "rough" things that have eclipsed our greatness, and finally we emerge as a rare jewel; a treasured vessel of GOD, fit for the Master's use and as splendid as a _Diamond!_

Thus, A Diamond in the Rough was written to **inspire** you to recognize your own value or brilliance, and understand that GOD is and has been working a work in and through you that will yield such a beneficial result that your life will glorify our Father, and be a blessing to the Kingdom of GOD.

It was also written to **instruct** you in some of the ways of GOD so that ultimately you will not fight the process, but instead you will learn how to embrace it and trust GOD even the more for your breakthrough and breakout!

And lastly, this book was penned to **ignite** a fire and passion in you that will cause you to go after your GOD ordained dreams, and to believe that Yes, GOD has chosen you to do great exploits on the earth that will advance His Kingdom, and cause you to live out your GOD given purposes!

So take out your pen and highlighter, and enjoy what GOD downloaded into me for you!

Chapter One

No Pressure ~ No Diamond!

*"We are hard-**pressed** on every side, yet not crushed; we are perplexed, but not in despair, persecuted, but not forsaken; struck down, but not destroyed...."*
2 Corinthians 4:8-9

My youngest son Malcolm, relating to his own experience of playing college football, simply said to me one day, *"Mom, no pressure, no diamond!"* At this point in his life he had come to the realization that pressure is all part of the development and formation process, and that without it; you will never yield a rewarding result! Without the pressure, diamonds would not be created...and without the trials and tests of life that pressure us, neither would vessels of honor fit for the Master's use!

Pressure can be defined as *"the exertion of force upon a surface by an object, fluid, etc. in contact with it; the use of persuasion, influence, or intimidation to make someone do something."* (Dictionary.com and Google dictionary) Pressure can come in a variety of ways, through different factors and via external forces. Pressure is typically unwelcomed, and oftentimes uninvited; yet in the end, if it is handled right, it can produce a desired result.

While diamonds are being formed under thousands of kilometers of the earth's crust, they undergo great levels of pressure and endure intensified levels of heat and temperatures that reach between 1600 to 2400 degrees Fahrenheit or greater. This intense heat, coupled with great pressure, works to help solidify the carbon atoms that form the diamond by developing its unique characteristics: size, shape and color. Without tons of pressure and intense temperatures, diamonds would not emerge with their exquisite properties and various hues that cause them to become the exquisite gems that they are. These distinct properties are the exact reason why the value of diamonds is so costly. The pressure and the heat, it seems, act as agents of transformation!

Fire Is A Purifier!

Similarly, when gold is being purified by fire, the dross and impurities that are within the metal compound are separated from the gold and refined away. Only what is true and authentic of this precious metal is able to stand the heat of the fire and is what emerges after the flames are turned off. The fire works as a purifier!

When we as Christians endure our own fiery trials, oftentimes our natural response is to complain, feel pity, and anxiously wait for its ending. However, if we submit to GOD as we endure the test, we may learn that the trial not only taught us something valuable, but it also burned away (if we let it) some carnal or fleshly ways that we may have relied on in the past as coping mechanisms. See, as a purifier, the fire can remove the dross or the unwanted flaws in our character, and leave behind the things that are good, noble and of good report. The fire may teach us how to trust the Lord more and complain less. It may purify our attitudes and enhance our faith. The fire, if we let it, can bring us out of the trial in better condition than when we went into it, if we recognize its purifying properties, and submit to the GOD that stands with us in the flames.

Pressure Has Purpose!

As servants of the Most High GOD with a great call on our lives; we too are introduced to the creative and transformative work of pressure and the purifying work of fire. Life's challenges, and the deprived nature of humanity, seem to work together at times to ensure that none of us escape the process of formation without experiencing pressure.

Pressure seems to drive us to the point where we are informed not only about the hidden qualities and coping mechanisms that we have developed over the years; but it also reveals to us and in us the areas that we are still challenged in emotionally, spiritually and psychologically. What is in us will undoubtedly come out of us when pressure is applied! Thus, pressure can be both **character building** and **character revealing.** Essentially, some things are not going to be revealed in us or to us until we are squeezed by circumstances and afflictions, or, like the diamond, until we are unfairly tossed into the heat of the fire...

In the Bible, Shadrach, Meshach and Abednego were also introduced to the faith-testing work of pressure and fiery trials. After standing for righteousness and refusing to bow down to an image of idol worship and egotism that King Nebuchadnezzar required of all citizens, the three Hebrew boys faced extreme pressure and opposition which eventually landed them into the fiery furnace. As Jews who were living in the province, they were required to follow the king's decree; yet Shadrach, Meshach and Abednego knew that they served the King of Kings, and thus they refused to bow before any other GOD.

The pressure to conform to the demands of their environment revealed their loyalty and commitment to their GOD. And despite the threat of the loss of their lives, the three Hebrew boys stood on their faith and declared that even if GOD decided not to save them from the fire, that He was still worthy to receive their sole allegiance and worship! Just like Jesus, they were telling the enemy to *"Get thee behind me satan, for it is written, You shall worship the Lord Your GOD, and Him only will you serve."(Luke 4:8)*

Shadrach, Meshach and Abednego refused to worship an image of idolatry and resisted the pressure to conform just to get along. The pressure revealed the true essence of their character, and the pressure revealed the true make-up of their being. Tossed into the furnace of affliction, the Hebrew boys did not flinch nor did they relent. They maintained their resolve to not compromise their faith. These tested servants who refused to bow emerged with a testimony of how GOD would always deliver them from every heated situation if they only trusted Him!

Saints of GOD, we need only to trust in the LORD and He will deliver us from every fiery trial!

Yes, there will be times in each of our lives when we will have to, like the Hebrew boys, stand on our principles and faith when we are in the heat of the battle, even though it may place us in harm's way or cause us to lose out on something that we really want. Although compromising to obtain some relief from the fire may seem tempting, in the end, being true to yourself and what you stand for will yield far greater results! If you are able to just hang on to your faith in GOD through the trial, you will realize that not only were you never alone in the furnace in the first place; but you will find that you have emerged with a greater anointing when it is all said and done! Because similar to the diamond, the pressure is forming and revealing your characteristics that authentically make up who you are!

Pressure Is Productive!

Air pressure in tires keeps our cars moving on the road...a pressurized cabin keeps the passengers safe while flying in an aircraft...and pressure that we face in our lives can produce much fruit if we don't grow weary! So you see, pressure can be productive!

Take the olive for example. The olive fruit, from which olive oil is extracted, endures a rigorous process of being strategically pressed in order to unveil its greatest and most useful commodity. In order for olive oil to be produced, the olive must endure the process of grinding and stay under the millstone for a specific length of time. A shorter grinding process may produce less oil; while a longer grinding process may reduce the flavor. Thus, a strategic and exact amount of time is needed to yield the anticipated outcome.

The oil, which is indicative of the Holy Spirit, is the precious desired result yielded from the various stages of pressure or crushing! And just as olive oil is produced from extreme and various amounts of pressure, so is the anointing in our lives increased through the numerous pressure cooking situations that we endure. Yes, pressure is productive, and the only way that you and I are going to be able to receive more of the anointing is by learning to handle more of the pressure! And the only way that we learn to handle more pressure is to spend more time with GOD in prayer, praise and feeding on His Word!

The anointing only comes through a supervised process by GOD whereby we are introduced to various amounts and degrees of resistance, disappointments, setbacks, letdowns, and even sometimes oppression and harassment.

When we find ourselves in the middle of a situation that causes us to feel constrained or hemmed in, that is the time that GOD is working in us to further develop us, mature us, and increase the anointing on our lives!

Just ask the Israelites as they left Egypt and felt the pressure of the Egyptians behind them and the Red Sea in front of them. Or ask Daniel when he was unfairly thrown into the lion's den, or the previously mentioned Hebrew boys.

When you are one of GOD'S chosen, *you will* face pressure situations. But the good news is that the pressure is never meant to kill you or your spirit, but it is there to make you stronger and grow you in your faith!

You grow in the anointing when you are pressured, as you learn to turn to GOD and His Word and His presence when life's circumstances begin to crush you. You realize that your methods are inadequate to get you through, and you learn to lean and depend on GOD to deliver you. He alone is the One that can part the Red Sea and take down the walls of Jericho in our lives. As we mature in our faith and seek GOD in the midst, we grow in the anointing and in His ways!

Similar to diamonds and olives, and parallel to the process that we must endure, pressure ultimately produces a valuable commodity!

Just as the pressure of the earth's weight impacts the diamond in its formation and causes it to reveal its brilliance and splendor, and just as an olive endures the weight of the millstone and the pressure applied to separate out the oil, so can the pressure of affliction and testing bring forth the best in us and produce a valuable outcome. **When we submit ourselves to GOD and allow the pressure to transform us and not deform us, greater levels of power, anointing and praise are produced in us that can be used mightily for Kingdom building!**

As servants of the Most High GOD, Shadrach, Meshach and Abednego allowed the pressure to be used productively and bring out the best of them; their faith in the Living GOD!

Ultimately, GOD wants us to know that the pressure that we endure as called out believers of Christ is designed to prepare us and subsequently promote us to new dimensions in Him so that we will effectively minister to others and witness great deliverances!

Pressure comes in many ways, shapes, sizes and forms. As its definition describes (on page 23), pressure can present as an exerting force, as harassment, or even the oppression that we experience because of situations or people that are pressing or compressing us. Sometimes pressure can also come as a constraining or compelling force or influence that desires to break us or cause us to bow down to its image or idols. Whatever way that pressure comes in your life, rest assured in knowing that it has purpose in your life and that ultimately GOD is working a work in you that is pressing out the dross and the impurities; and only leaving what is authentic! As Creator of the Universe, GOD is creating a brilliant work of art in and through us that is valuable and precious like a diamond!

Develop a thick skin, but maintain a soft heart!

One of the most valuable coping mechanisms' that is learned from handling a great amount of pressure is developing tough skin. When oppression and force are being greatly applied to your life through adversity or trials, developing or obtaining "thick skin" is an acquired skill that will serve you well in your walk. For "thick skin" allows you to feel the pinch from life's trials and tribulations, but it anesthetizes you from the sting! In other words, you will be able to stand in the fire, but honey, you won't even get burned!

The key to handling this amount of pressure and affliction and still emerging useful for GOD is to learn to develop a thick skin; *but to maintain a soft heart!*

Saints of GOD, this is where the true test lies. For when we find ourselves like David in Psalm 40 being surrounded by innumerable enemies, our first response is not typically to walk in maturity. If the truth be told, many other thoughts may plague our minds before we reason that we will not allow our enemies to "take" us there! It is during these times that we can learn to develop tough skin and allow the darts being thrown to hit our armor, but not our hearts. I'm not going to lie; this time is tricky! Because, if you are not careful, while your skin is toughening, your heart can also be hardening which will cause you to become ineffective in your work for GOD! It takes skill to allow the skin to toughen, while keeping your heart soft and pliable. This is only accomplished by staying in the Word of GOD and in the face of GOD through prayer and submission! Believers, it is only when we stay in the face of GOD that we will learn how to take a licking and keep on ticking!

While in the process of writing this book, I found myself in a situation orchestrated by a third party in an effort to cause a rift between me and another woman of GOD. The whole event was manipulated and the story that emerged was twisted and turned to cast me in a bad light. Unfortunately, the other sister was in a vulnerable state at the time in her life, so she believed the concocted story and lies and refused to hear me out. I refused to give in to the trap and engage in a debate because GOD had revealed to me what was at the core of it all, but the person continued accusing me of something I clearly did not do. All the while that this scenario was playing out, GOD would not allow me to defend myself or reveal who I knew was behind the strife.

Despite my frustration with it all and the subsequent dismissive attitude of the deceived sister afterwards, GOD would not allow me to respond in anger. He only allowed me to pray for the sister being manipulated who was operating out of manufactured anger. For weeks I prayed and continued to show love to this sister in Christ until love prevailed and the manufactured strife that she wrongfully held against me dissipated. A few weeks later, this same woman of GOD confirmed for me what I had already known through revelation; that there was a third party instigator who was behind the whole thing! I remember contemplating while it was all going on, "GOD why are you allowing this deceiver to seemingly prosper in her plans?" However, at the end I was the better for it; for I found that I did not *react* to the situation, but GOD graced me to *respond* to it in love. I trusted GOD as it unfolded. And while I could not say a mumbling word in my defense, my heart did not become hard, my skin grew tougher, and thanks be to GOD...I maintained a soft heart.

Friends, an increased love walk is needed to operate at this level! Learning how to love the people that the enemy is using in your life to attack you is not easy, but it is possible. Especially when you sincerely pray for them and GOD allows you to see that they are hurting and only reacting out of their condition. It is true...hurting people do hurt people!

There are times when I still fall short in this area, and that is when GOD reminds me through Ephesians 4:1-3 to *"...walk worthy of the calling with which you were called, with all lowliness and gentleness, with longsuffering, bearing with one another in love, endeavoring to keep the unity of the Spirit in the bond of peace."*

It is important to remain poised when attacks come. Prepare your heart daily in the Word, praise and prayer, and remain low and gentle with others; especially those that rub you the wrong way. Maturing in the LORD and increasing your love walk with Him allows you to be able to pray for those that are like sandpaper in your life. It teaches you to hope for their best because they are a soul desperately in need of GOD'S love; just as you are!

Give up the right to be right for the right to walk in righteousness!

People of GOD, we cannot afford to lose ground or separate ourselves from the Master's voice by carrying unforgiveness, bitterness, anger and frustration in our hearts. When we find ourselves under great pressure and in the heat of the battle, this is the time that we must learn to *give up the right to be right, for the right to walk in GOD's righteousness!*

Giving up the right to be right means learning how to hold your peace and allow GOD to fight your battles. We must learn to turn that offense, turn that lie that they told on you, turn that anger over their deceptive plots and plans over to GOD and allow Him to work it out. Meanwhile, you stay focused, stay in peace, and stay in right relationship with GOD. In the end, it is truly not worth winning the point over, only to find out that you have lost the entire match!

When we stay in bitterness over an offense, it only hurts us. Trust me, that other person has most likely moved on, but you remain bound and unable to operate in the fullness of GOD because your heart is carrying the spirit of offense. Even if what they did to you was wrong and it hurt, refuse to allow them to further abuse you by not forgiving them and staying in strife. Turn them and the offense over to GOD, and you stay free!

Pressure is a complicated and multi-faceted tool. In some ways it is a unique driving force that can also be considered a double-edged sword. For you see, pressure can simultaneously be painful *and* productive; provoking *and* yet prolific. Pressure can cause us to react, affect us physically and emotionally, and push us to act in uncharacteristic ways if we are not careful. However, pressure can also, if we let it, develop in us a mental and emotional toughness that is needed if we are truly going to inherit the promises of GOD and press towards the mark of the high calling in Christ Jesus!

GOD told Joshua several times to be strong in the LORD and to be of good courage as he led GOD's people to the Promised Land! When pressure is applied, we need to learn to be strong in GOD's might and not in our own, and allow Him to develop in us the fortitude to walk this journey out with grace and in love!

Yes, my friend, pressure can be painful and anxiety producing when we experience great amounts of it; but if we stay totally surrendered to the Master through cultivating an intimate relationship with him, we will surely be led into our purpose.... if we do not try to exit the **process**....

Chapter Two

In The Process of Time!

*"And it came to pass in **process of time**..."*
Exodus 2:23

Diamonds evolve through the process of time. Beginning as a lump of carbon and then emerging into a precious jewel, the formation process of a diamond is both transformative and effective! Just think of it ...after enduring great heat and tremendous amounts of pressure, in the fullness of time, volcanic activity works to push diamonds to the earth's surface where they are mined and collected.

Thousands of years transpire before a lump of carbon is transformed into a precious, costly gem! Great pressure, extreme temperatures, and an extensive amount of time are needed in the formation of this precious jewel!

After all, a quality product must undergo a rigorous process in order for it to fulfill its destined purpose at the appropriate time!

Akin to diamonds, butterflies go through a formative process called a metamorphosis in which they leave their natural state as a caterpillar and emerge into a colorful masterpiece of the Creator! It is during this time of transition that the butterfly remains encapsulated, or in a seeming "holding pattern" while it is developing, maturing and being transformed into its new likeness. Freed from its caterpillar phase of crawling on its belly, but not yet liberated into its new life of flying and soaring, this insect is held suspended in the air in a "holding pattern" until its fullness of time comes.

II Corinthians 3:18

"But we all, with open face beholding as in a glass the glory of the Lord, are changed into the same image from glory to glory, even as by the Spirit of the Lord."

A few summers ago, my friends and I were headed off to a beach in New Jersey, and as we got off the exit for the beach my girlfriend noticed a sign for a Live Butterfly Garden. Knowing that I love butterflies and that GOD uses them in my life in various ways, my girlfriend Renee announced that we were taking a detour to the Butterfly Garden. Upon entering the gift shop attached to the Garden, we were introduced to one of the owners and he gave us a guided tour into the exhibit. The minute that we walked into the exhibit, we instantly stopped and began to weep as we felt the presence of the Lord and experienced the beauty and serenity of that environment. Butterflies began to greet us and flutter around us as we entered into their sacred space. While touring the exhibit we witnessed various types and hues of butterflies. We were privileged to watch a set of butterflies mating, and we were even blessed with the opportunity to observe a butterfly give birth as she gently laid an egg on a tree branch.

Out of all the beauty that we witnessed and experienced that day, what eventually spoke to us the loudest was when the exhibits' owner showed us through the window the area where the cocoons or Chrysalis were hanging. Row upon row, we observed the hanging cocoons where the caterpillars were incubating before becoming butterflies. There was no movement and really nothing spectacular to behold. However, the revelation that we received from watching these cocoons was that these forming butterflies were segregated and set apart from the rest of the butterflies in their own sacred space. Their space was tailor made for them and had to be under the right, specific conditions to afford them the opportunity to become what they were created and designed to become. Although these future butterflies were in a holding pattern as they matured, the proper environment was key to their successful development. This cocoon process, although complicated and intricate, was hidden from the world in obscurity as GOD transformed these previously earth bound creatures into ones that would be liberated and fly with grace and ease.

We further learned on that day that while the butterflies are incubating within the cocoon, a transformative process is taking place where their juvenile structures are broken down and their adult structures are being formed. Their juvenile bone structure that successfully supported them as caterpillars is no longer sufficient to sustain them and their weight as butterflies Thus, a maturity process is needed for their bones just to support the newness of their role and being!

As GOD's children, we are sanctified daily for His use and His glory. Similar to the caterpillar, we too are "set apart" unto GOD. This "setting apart" involves GOD transforming us more into His image when we are submitted unto Him. We are constantly being developed and matured to grow in Him. Similar to the butterfly, we too go through confined situations and periods of isolation whereby GOD in His infinite wisdom, uses that time to break down our "juvenile structures" or immature ways, and He develops in us "adult structures" or maturity to handle the new role, the new promotion, the new person that we are becoming in Him. The old ways, the old coping mechanisms are no longer sufficient for us and will not work in the newness that He is bringing us into. Like the caterpillar, we too have to transform into something that will be able to handle the weight of our new assignments. Where in the past we might have reacted to great pressure in carnal or fleshly ways, GOD uses our cocoon moments to work in us His Spirit, His responses, and His ways! Our seeming "holding patterns" have great reward if we submit to what GOD is doing, and if we do not try to exit the process before the work is done!

A few weeks after visiting the Butterfly Garden my girlfriend Durelle and I were talking about our experience, and it was at this precise moment that I came to the revelation in my own life that GOD had recently placed me in a "holding pattern" in which I could no longer operate in the former, familiar places of my life and ministry; however, I was not yet released into the new season or things of my life. Feeling somewhat suspended between seasons, I realized that I was not able to go back to what was comfortable and common to me; and yet I was also unable to walk into the new realm and spheres that GOD was showing me. I was being held up in a spiritual cocoon of transformation and unable to take my cues from anyone but Him.

As a Christian that is called according to GOD'S purpose, you will experience a transformative process in Christ in which GOD separates you unto Himself and places you in a "holding pattern" while he breaks down your juvenile structures or immature ways and develops in you more adult or mature structures, all in preparation for your release or launching into your destined purpose! For it is all about your divine PURPOSE!

And said unto them, Ye [are] the chief of the fathers of the Levites: sanctify yourselves, [both] ye and your brethren, that ye may bring up the ark of the LORD GOD of Israel unto [the place that] I have prepared for it. (1 Chronicles 15:12)

Yes, we all experience change at the time of salvation, but there is also a time of purification whereby GOD begins to sanctify you and set you apart for the work that He has prepared for you to do.

In the book of Esther, its namesake experienced the same process that I am referring to as GOD began to set her apart to become Queen and eventually save her people and future generations from genocide. Taken away from her family and community and then being thrust into a life of preparation with other virgins in a foreign place, Esther's purification process began to prepare her to be presented favorably to the king. This year-long process of preparation in obscurity equipped Esther mentally, physically, and spiritually to be ready to walk into the role of a queen if chosen above all others.

The process takes place as GOD prepares you for what He has already prepared for you!

During this preparation process, Esther entered her own type of "holding pattern" whereby she could not go back to her former life with her uncle Mordecai, but yet she had not been chosen for her new life as Queen. Housed in the palace, GOD began preparing Esther for her future in obscurity; away from her family, friends, and all that was familiar to her. However, after a year, the fullness of time had come for the king to select his new wife, and Esther was favored above all and chosen as Queen thereby releasing her into her purpose, and ultimately her life's destiny. Esther survived the process, and now she had been elevated to the role that she had ultimately been prepared for!

In the year 2011, Catherine "Kate" Middleton experienced a time of preparation for her pending new role as the wife of British royalty, Prince William. Kate was prepped on royal protocol and regal social graces, and she endured a process of preparation that equipped her to be the wife of an heir apparent to the British throne. The process, as it were, readied her for a historic position and enabled her to flow gracefully into her new role as the Duchess of Cambridge.

The process is a time of preparation and separation that ultimately prepares you for your time of elevation. In other words, the process takes place as GOD prepares <u>*you*</u> for what GOD has already prepared <u>*for you*</u>!

The mere fact that you are going through some sort of process with GOD should elicit joy and hope in your heart. It affirms that GOD is preparing you with intention; and that all of the hard times and all of the stretching is not haphazard, but it is purposeful and bringing you to an expected end!

A great purpose requires great preparation...and great preparation involves a great process!

The Gospel teaches us that Jesus was born under scrutiny and death threats. His family had to flee with him to Egypt until the evil King Herod was dead. At the tender age of twelve, our Savior re-emerged on the scene and was found reasoning with teachers in the temple and eager to be about His Father's business. Despite His zeal, our Savior was brought back home again to continue to be subject to His parents while *"Jesus increased in wisdom and stature, and in favor with GOD and man (Luke 2:52)."* During this time, Jesus endured His process in obscurity. It would be another 18 years before Jesus would emerge again. Some may argue that Jesus' 30 year process in obscurity further prepared Him for His 3 years of powerful ministry in public!

Jesus' lengthy process of increasing in wisdom and stature and in favor with GOD and man prepared Him for His most powerful and eternal purpose...to redeem fallen humanity back to our loving and just GOD!

Jesus' purpose was the greatest of all time; and it required a very long period of preparation. As humans we are often impatient and desire instant gratification. But a great purpose requires great preparation... and great preparation involves a great process! We must be willing to endure the extensive duration of our process if we are ever going to be mature enough to enjoy the expansive blessing of walking in our purpose!

II Corinthians 5:17 teaches us that *"if any man be in Christ he is a new creature: old things are passed away, behold all things are become new."* Just as the diamond and the butterfly experience great conversions and adaptations in their processes, we as children of the Most High GOD also experience significant transformations as we go through ours! Every one of us who are living on purpose for purpose and are in relationship with our Lord and Savior Jesus Christ have entered into the "process" whereby GOD allows His transformative work to change us from "glory to glory" and conform us to His image! *"But we all, with open face beholding as in a glass that glory of the Lord, are changed into the same image from glory to glory, even as by the Spirit of the Lord." (2 Corinthians 3:18)*

IN THE PROCESS OF TIME

If we pause and take the time to look back over our journey thus far with the Lord, I am sure that each one of us can see GOD's hand at work in our lives as He has brought us through various situations, experiences, trials and triumphs! Every step of the way, GOD has been orchestrating our lives through a process that is meant to not only draw us closer to Him, but to purge away the things that would hold us back as He prepares us for a greater work.

This process that GOD takes us through is also known as sanctification, and it is a lifetime work. None of us will ever "arrive" or be perfected until Jesus takes us home. However, throughout our process of sanctification we will experience innumerable tests that will challenge us in our development and that will subsequently prepare us for promotion when we master them.

Like the diamond, as we submit ourselves to this "process" GOD slowly chisels away at the carbon (the carnal weight) in our lives through the pressure and conditions of life, and He reveals more of His glory or brilliance in us. As we continue to submit to our Father, we emerge into spectacular vessels that not only understand our value and self-worth, but who also shine so bright that we bring glory to GOD and His Kingdom! *After all, we are King's kids!*

It can be hard and challenging when we are in the process. However, while we are going through our process and test, it is comforting to know that GOD promises to never leave us or forsake us! And if we take the time to pause and reflect over this promise, we will realize that our Father has been right there with us all along overseeing the entire progression. And not only has He been overseeing the process, but just like Job, GOD has prescribed certain boundaries and timeframes around our pressure cooking situations; and in the fullness of time, yes, the test will be over!

"Although the test seems unbearable, you are surviving it!"

In 2009, I went for an MRI test as ordered by my doctor. I remember experiencing some anxiety prior to the test because I was not looking forward to spending any length of time in this enclosed space, which in my opinion, welcomes the feeling of claustrophobia. Prior to going into the actual machine I was given various instructions that I needed to know in preparation for the exam. First, the technician informed me that they would be taking a series of images that would be administered in varying increments. Next, she stated that I would have to be very still while the test was being given. Thirdly, I was informed that they would bring me back out of the machine halfway through the test to administer a dye into my bloodstream.

After that, she stated that I would hear her voice over the loud speaker as the test progressed. And lastly, that she would be providing me with a buzzer to hold in my hand that would afford me the opportunity to signal her and advise her with urgency if I had the need to come out of the machine. I was then drawn into the machine and the *process* began...

The technician began photographing a series of images and announced before each series how many minutes each segment would take. She would announce, "This image will take 3 minutes. Please remain still," and then time would elapse. She would then come back over the speaker and state, "This next one will be 5 minutes in length" and then..."6 minutes"...and so on. What I began to shortly realize after a few moments was that although the entire process would take over 45 minutes (which is a long time when you are shut up in a tight machine); the test was definitely more bearable being administered in these palatable increments!

What I also discovered was that after every series, the technician would make an encouraging comment like, "You are doing well.

Just a few more images. You are doing great!" This break up of timing, coupled with statements of affirmation throughout the testing procedure, provided me with some relief as it made the testing procedure more tolerable and manageable. Every time that I began to feel like I couldn't stand another minute in that robotic coffin, the technician would announce the ending of that particular series and offer a word of encouragement that was meant to ground me in the truth that although the test seemed unbearable, *I was surviving it!* And you too can survive any test that comes your way! Know that in the midst of your trial or your test that GOD is in control, and He is watching and timing the experience; and an end is near.

GOD does the same thing for us when we are in the midst of our test or fiery furnace; because He alone knows how much we can truly bear. For just when we are about to give up in the middle of some trial, some conflict, or some problem, He gives us an indication that the test will soon be over and that we are enduring this hardship as a good soldier and that we are faring well!

Although the test may be hard, and although it may take us out of our comfort zone, GOD is still saying "well done!" He already knew all along that we would be able to bear it because He has built us to last!

In the movie I, Robot with Will Smith, at the climax of the picture the robot Sunny is sent on a mission to save the universe. To do so, Sunny has to place his robotic arm through intense radioactive waves to disarm the out of control computer. The arms of the regular robots would have easily disintegrated due to their chemical makeup. But after Sunny puts his arm in and successfully disarms the computer, he turns to the others and states, "My father built me with denser alloy...I guess this was my purpose!" Sunny understood that his father built him with materials that would enable him to last as he fulfilled his purpose; where others would not have. And GOD has done the same thing for us. He has built us to last through all of the storms, all of the trials, all of the tribulations, and even the process. We have been built by our Father to last!!!

"No temptation has overtaken you except which is common to man, but GOD is faithful, who will not allow you to be tempted beyond what you are able, but with the temptation will also make the way of escape, that you may be able to bear it!"
1 Corinthians 10:13

This word "temptation" in the Greek is translated as *"test or trial"*. Thus, GOD's Word in 1 Corinthians 10:13 clearly tells us that GOD is not going to allow us to be tested beyond what we are able to handle, but that with the trial GOD has already made a way of out for us that we would be able to bear or stand up under it.

GOD knows our frame and that we are mere dust. He also knows our breaking point. In Psalm 30:9 David asks GOD how can I praise You when I am in the pit (of despair). He goes on to ask, *"Will the dust...will it declare Your truth?"* David was reminding GOD of how hard the pit periods are and that in those times it can be hard to praise Him. David learned a valuable lesson through his pit *processing* time, for Psalm 30 is being written by David for the dedication of the temple; which means that he fulfilled his purpose. David learned that through it all, the pit was only preparing him for his promotion! *Hallelujah!*

That is what times of testing do. They measure for us our preparedness for the next level or dimension. Think about it. When you were in school, after you finished studying the lessons and your notes, it was time for the test. And after the final exam, then came the promotion to the next grade or level! Tests are an indication that advancement is coming!

IN THE PROCESS OF TIME

After the MRI test was over and I had a chance to think about it, I realized that as comforting as the time announcements and the consoling statements were from the technician, the most liberating part of the whole testing process for me was knowing that even if I had become extremely anxious and could no longer bear the claustrophobic feeling, that the technician had provided me with a way of escape before the test had even started. For I always knew that the buzzer that she provided to me was an available escape route if I needed it! Despite the tight space, the anxiety over the test, the feeling of being closed in a coffin, I took comfort in knowing that I always, always had an exit strategy at my disposal if need be! *Praise the Lord!*

GOD is the ultimate Creator...He knows how much force, how much time, and how much pressure is needed to mold us and make us into a beautiful and useful vessel! Therefore my brothers and sisters in Christ, the tests that we are taking are controlled tests administered by the greatest Proctor, our Lord and Savior Jesus Christ! We need not worry about how long the test that we are in is going to last. We just simply need to trust the Timekeeper!

My friends, our process will not be complete until the Lord brings us home, and just as diamonds continue to need cleaning and care, so will we! Yet there will be a fullness of time in our process whereby we will emerge from the confined boundaries of our spiritual cocoons knowing and displaying the brilliance of who GOD created us to be. We will emerge with an understanding of GOD's original design and intent for our lives and we will begin living on purpose and for purpose because of GOD's transformative power working in our lives!

What we emerge with will be costly; and who we emerge as will be more precious than a diamond! And as we emerge...all will be able to see our splendor and attest to the conversion that has taken place in our lives similar to the butterfly. Refusing to crawl another day, we will soar in the liberty that we have obtained in and through the process that GOD has taken us!

The process is never about punishment, it's only about purpose!

The process at times may seem hard, lonely, lengthy and oppressive, and throughout it we may even question whether GOD is still there or if He even knows what He is doing. There are points when we may even offer as Jesus did; for GOD to take this cup from us. Yet, because we know our purpose, and we trust the One who called us, we will conclude as Jesus did, "Nevertheless, not my will, but yours be done!"

There was a time in ministry that I found myself being misunderstood, my character being assassinated, and my loyalty being discredited; but GOD would not allow me to speak in my defense. This period reminded me of when our Savior was being wrongfully accused. My obedience and service to Him was being misconstrued, and all the while I was not allowed to offer a defense. I did not know how things would turn out, but I did know that the same GOD Who brought me to this level of persecution would bring me through it. I had to learn to trust the GOD of the process even though the process seemed to be betraying me. It was then that I learned that *the process is never, never about punishment, it's only about purpose,* to produce a good and expected end! (Jeremiah 29:11)

Child of GOD, the process of transformation may make you question the call, and yes, even the Caller. It may challenge every bit of your faith and cause you to want to retreat and go back to the life you lived before you accepted the call. As you push your way through the process, you may find that the pressure and unrelenting attacks may even cause you to get angry at GOD!

But the process is not meant to offend us or cause us to feel like GOD has it in for us. Quite the contrary, the process is meant to prepare us and equip us to live our destined lives on purpose! It is out of GOD's love for us that He supervises and orchestrates our process so that we can come to maturity and fulfill the calling and assignments for which He created us!

Go through it and Grow through it!

GOD desires for each and every one of us in Christ to hear the most coveted greeting of *"Well done thy good and faithful servant, enter into the joy of thy Lord!" (Matthew 25:21)* And in order for us to be considered as a faithful servant, we must go through our servant formation process of development and maturation to equip us for the Masters' use. Believers, the process is ultimately about growth, and even our Savior was not exempt!

There are many levels and there can be more than one calling in your lifetime. Thus, there will be numerous tests that you experience. But as you begin to get more understanding, you will discover that when you truly embrace the process, you are embracing more of the King and His Kingdom, and more of the destined life that

He created for you before the world began. With maturity we learn to accept the test and trials as they come. We have to *go* through it and *grow* through it; but ultimately we know that GOD is working a work in us for our good and for His glory.

People of GOD, *the process takes place as GOD prepares you for what He has already prepared for you!* Submit to the process, learn lifetime lessons in the process, and emerge as a beautifully transformed creation willing to serve the LORD fully committed. Yes, the process may be grueling, but remember it is timed and that GOD ultimately has control over the buzzer!

GOD birthed you with purpose; watches over His Word in your life to perform it; and subjects you to the process to ensure that a dividend is yielded from His investment. When we say yes to GOD's will, He watches over the Word that He spoke in each of our lives to ensure that it will manifest and come to pass!

The Bible declares in Genesis 8:22 that *"While the earth remaineth, seedtime and harvest...shall not cease."* There are some scholars that believe that the word "seedtime" should be separated and written as two distinct words in this passage; "seed" and "time". Because what takes place between the moment that seeds are planted, and the actual occurrence of when the harvest is manifested, is time! And during that duration is when a process takes place. The process entails the seed being subjected to conditions that assist in transforming it into its intended outcome; its intended purpose! *The process takes time...*

Many people desire greatness but they refuse to submit to the process to become a vessel that can be used greatly for GOD! The pain of the pressure, coupled with the prolonged duration of the process is what normally causes people to retreat. Typically, it is not a lack of desire that makes people give up – but a lack of perseverance when things get tough! This is the time that we must learn to **Persevere, and fight for our future...**

Chapter Three

Perseverance: Fighting for Your Future

*"Because you have kept My command to **persevere**, I also will keep you from the hour of trial which shall come upon the whole world, to test those who dwell on earth."*
(Revelation 3:10)

In order for diamonds to break through and surface on the earth's plain during a volcanic eruption, they must first press past multiple layers of the earth's substance in order to be mined and discovered as precious jewels. They fight their way through rocks, around sediment, pushing past the earth's mantle and its crust to finally emerge successfully to the earth's surface. Despite all of the hindering elements in their way during the discharge of a volcano, diamonds emerge through all of the dirt to break through the barriers and reach a place of discovery! It is at this place of discovery where the brilliance of a diamond is unearthed and recognized in all its greatness! Similar to diamonds, we as GOD'S children are often hindered by things that may block us or stand in the way of our liberty or our freedom. Oftentimes our brilliance is hidden beneath layers of seemingly immovable barriers that prevent us from coming to a place of discovering our inherent worth and value. Just like the diamond, it often takes circumstances compareable to a volcanic eruption to cause us to push past all of the hindrances in our lives and emerge victorious on top of it all; in all of our GOD given splendor and glory!

In the Gospel of Matthew 26:6-13, we find the story of Mary of Bethany. Mary is with Jesus and His disciples at Simon the Leper's house when she begins to anoint Jesus' head with costly perfume poured out of an alabaster flask. Outraged by this act, the disciples begin to protest and question why, in their opinion, Mary would waste such an expensive fragrance instead of selling it and giving the money to the poor. Learning of their protests, Jesus interjects and questions His disciples as to why they are troubling Mary since she has *"done a good work for Me."* Jesus goes on to tell them that, unlike Him, they will have the poor with them always, but that this woman was preparing Him for His burial! As Jesus further affirms Mary's actions,

He adds that wherever in the world this Gospel is preached, that what Mary has done will be spoken of as a memorial to her! Mary's actions earned her a prestigious place in Biblical history. What is it that we can learn from Mary's actions?

Push Past the Dirt!

When we review the text carefully we can note that Mary employed three very key strategies in this moment. Let's consider...

First, Mary defied her detractors and *pushed past the dirt* of the objections that they were slinging her way!

Mary could have easily allowed their words and disdain to cause her to abandon her display of love to her Savior. But instead of allowing their words and looks to stop her or block her, Mary pushed past their dirt and remained focused. Mary refused to allow their objections to offend her...she refused to allow their protest to paralyze her...and she refused to allow them to keep her from preparing her Savior for His purpose. And because Mary did, we are discussing her actions now; thousands of years later.

Secondly, Mary *continued on her course and in her calling.* Yes, after pushing past the dirt, Mary did not get side tracked, and she continued fulfilling her GOD given mission!

Mary continued to go forth with anointing Jesus' head because she knew this was her GOD given purpose and her calling. I believe Mary recognized that she had a charge to keep and a GOD to glorify; and her perseverance allowed her to fulfill her destiny despite their distractions. And because she refused to be stopped and she refused to be turned around from her course of action, *Mary was privileged to participate in a divine event that had eternal implications!* This was Mary's third accomplishment!

Mary's refusal to allow those who were not privy to the instructions that GOD had given her to cause her to retreat afforded her a once in an eternity opportunity to participate in a historical encounter. **Mary prepared the Savior of the world for His death, burial and resurrection!** ***Hallelujah!!!***

You see, GOD gives each of us instruction and directions in our life to lead us to our destined place, and the conversation is an isolated one; only between us and GOD. The people that are trying to distract you and derail your future were not privy to that conversation between you and GOD, so they don't know the plans that GOD has for you to prosper you and bring you to a future and a hope! So we cannot allow these same uninformed people to stop us from fulfilling our calling, simply because they don't know it.

Pharaoh did not know he would be caring for a deliverer when he allowed Moses to be brought into the kingdom...Saul didn't know that he was chasing the next king to replace him when he set out to kill David...and the chief priests and the scribes did not believe that they were crucifying the Savior when they hung Him high and stretched Him wide!

People of GOD, our detractors do not know who we are or how we are called to participate in GOD's plan. So we must do as Jesus did and pray the prayer, "Father, forgive them, for they know not what they do!" For in reality, when they come against GOD's plans in our lives; they are really coming against His divine will. And ultimately, the battle is not ours; it's the Lords!

You see, in ancient Israel, burial practices were a sacred tradition. As part of the burial practices after the death of a loved one, family members would mourn and prepare the body for burial. The deceased's body was washed and anointed with various oils and spices before being wrapped in linen and placed in the tomb. Undoubtedly familiar with the burial practices of the day, Mary's actions were not only affirming her faith in who Jesus was, but she was also making a declaration of His purpose and why He came. For she knew that just as Jesus had taught her previously when she laid at His feet over at her sister Martha's house as recorded in Luke 10:39, that He would suffer many things and be killed as a Lamb slain for the salvation of the world. Ultimately, Mary's worship was an exercise of her faith in action that Jesus truly was the Messiah. Mary's faith met her works, and she accomplished a divine feat that we are beneficiaries of today. Mary's perseverance in the face of her detractors garnered her a place in the Gospel Memorial!

What will our faith render us as we overcome the voices of dissension from our detractors?

Mary's actions were key to her fulfilling her GOD given destiny and they are also key lessons for us if we are ever going to be able to fulfill our destiny and take part in something significant for the King and His Kingdom!

We must like Mary, set our hearts to push past the dirt that others try to place on us from their own mess, and fulfill what GOD has created for us to do. Whatever problem they have with you fulfilling your call in Christ is their issue; it is their problem; it is their dirt! Push past it!!!

Trailblazers don't stop on the side of the road to listen to detractors. They continue on their path in the face of objection!

Pushing past the objections of others is the only way that we are going to be able to *continue on the course* that GOD has set us on *and fulfill our calling* in Him. Learning how to push past the people who are counting us out and trying to dismiss us will be easy to do once we realize that while they are counting us out; *Jesus is counting us in!*

When the disciples sternly objected to Mary's actions and were speaking against her fulfilling her purpose, Jesus took up for Mary and affirmed her, even when her display of love for Jesus disagreed with the majority!

We cannot allow the objections or distractions of others to cause us to back up or retreat before we fulfill what GOD has called us to do. Trailblazers don't stop on the side of the road to listen to detractors. They continue on their path in the face of objection!

Remaining determined to complete our assignment will not only demonstrate our level of obedience to GOD, but it may also open up the door for someone else to fulfill their purpose and calling too! For when we refuse to shrink back in fear or give in to intimidation, we unconsciously give others the permission to do the same!

Children of GOD, we won't know the true significance or impact that our obedience to GOD's instructions will have until and unless we actually surrender and obey. Our obedience may actually lead to us being able to participate in an event that has eternal implications for the Kingdom's sake. We may never fully know how GOD will choose to use us, but we can ensure that we are open and available to be used!

Pushing past the dirt is a way of fighting for your future. Refusing to be sidetracked on your way to your destiny is all a part of the process.

In the book of Exodus, GOD declared to the Israelites that they would one day inherit the Promised Land; a land flowing with milk and honey. GOD painted a wonderful picture of what Canaan would look like and He assured them that He was bringing them into the Promised Land because He was their GOD and they were His people. GOD showed them their inheritance and their future! However, what GOD neglected to tell them at the time was that they would first have to endure slavery at the hands of Pharaoh; wander 40 years in the wilderness; and then have to fight and dispossess all the "ites" in the land before they would ever be able to inherit the

Promise. GOD told them about Canaan, but He did not tell them about the Canaanites! *The Israelites had to fight for their future!*

"Warfare always precedes the Promise, and the Wilderness always precedes the Promised Land"

Whatever GOD has promised you in your life you must remember that it will not come easy and that you will have to fight for it before you can inherit it. The Promise that GOD has made to each of us will come to pass! However, the road that we must take to inherit it or occupy it will include hard work and the need to persevere through battles and trials!

The word "occupy" literally means to dispossess and then possess. Thus, in order for us to be able to occupy the places of our inheritance, we will first have to dispossess the enemies that are illegitimately inheriting our promise! Truly, one of the ways that you can know that you are getting ready to inherit GOD'S promises in your life is by taking inventory of the number of "ites" that you will have to fight in a given season!

You literally will find yourself fighting for your future at every turn and on every hand; but know this, that GOD will undoubtedly grace you for the battle, and He will place fortitude in you that will not allow you to give up!

The Israelites path to their Promised Land included them journeying through the land of the Hittites, the Hivites, the Perizzites, the Gergashites, the Amorites and the Jebusites. They had to travel through the enemy's territory and fight their way to and through Canaan in order for them to inherit what GOD already had given them.

The Israelites' journey reminds us that warfare always precedes the promise, and the wilderness always precedes us getting to the Promised Land!

Nehemiah, the Old Testament leader, is a wonderful example of fighting for your future and persevering for your purpose...

Nehemiah was in exile under King Artaxerxes, and he was serving as the king's cupbearer when he became distressed over learning about the condition of his homeland Jerusalem and its walls. Being granted permission and favor by the king, Nehemiah heads to Jerusalem to repair the walls and bring restoration back to his native land. As Nehemiah and many of the Jews had a mind to work and began rebuilding the wall, instantly opposition arose from two pagan officials named Sanballat and Tobiah. Jealous because of the good work that Nehemiah was doing, Sanballat and Tobiah conspired and schemed to try to hinder, frustrate and destroy the restorative work that Nehemiah and his people were achieving. Yet in the face of learning of their plot, Nehemiah did not relent from his purpose, but instead, he so calmly responded *"Nevertheless we made our prayer to our GOD, and because of them we set a watch against them day and night."(Nehemiah 4:9)*

Once Nehemiah learned of Sanballat's and Tobias' diabolical schemes, he did not complain, moan or send a message to the king. Instead, Nehemiah knew to go to the His heavenly Father in prayer!

"Watch and pray, lest you enter into temptation!"

When we are working a work for the Lord and are confronted with intimidated manipulative people, our first response cannot be to turn to the arm of flesh, for their help is limited. No, our first response must be to turn and bombard heaven with strategic prayers and then set a watch against the enemy's subtle attacks!

The Bible trains us in Matthew 26:41 to *"Watch and pray, lest you enter into temptation..."* When we are facing opposition from the enemy for righteousness sake and we are fighting for our future, we must employ our weapons of warfare that are not carnal and that can pull down strongholds in the heavenlies! Prayer is an effective weapon and it allows us to persevere through when the heat of antagonism from the enemy is on.

It can be so tempting to react in the flesh to people who are being used by the enemy. Especially with those that proverbially rub us the wrong way. But if we take a lesson from Nehemiah, we will quickly learn that GOD is a great avenger and that when we seek GOD in prayer and release our enemies to Him, He will defend us, and He will resolve the matter.

Nehemiah's quick employment of prayer when he was approached with negativity is a sign of a mature, great leader who is effectively trained in the art of warfare. When engaged in spiritual warfare, a true warrior knows that not only must you pray, but you must also watch and be alert for any additional tricks of the enemy. So Nehemiah positioned his men!

Nehemiah positioned his men on the wall and never took his eyes off of his work as he prayed. In fact, Nehemiah and the men that worked on the wall carried tools with one hand and a weapon with the other. They continued to work and they did not allow their construction to be halted as they remained positioned to fight!

Take the high road and refuse to descend!

As a leader, Nehemiah not only mastered how to persevere through unjustified attacks, but he also mastered how to stay focused when the enemy comes to distract you and try to take you off course when you are doing a great work!

When Sanballat and Tobiah sent a letter of intimidation to Nehemiah that was filled with lies in an attempt to get him to stop his progress, Nehemiah responded to their communication of fear by sending his people with the following message, *"I am doing a great work, so that I cannot come down. Why should the work cease while I leave it and go down to you?"* *(Nehemiah 6:3)*

Nehemiah let them know that he refused to come down to their level to deal with some foolishness designed to derail him and distract him from the great work that he was doing for GOD!

Just like Mary, Nehemiah stayed focused on his assignment and purpose and never gave in to the distractions and intimidation. Children of GOD, whatever assignment you have been given by the Lord to complete in this season, don't allow the enemy to distract you and take your focus so that you will not finish the good work that has been entrusted to your hands.

As I began to write this book in obedience to GOD, I faced a Nehemiah attack by the enemy that was orchestrated in an attempt to steal my focus and cause me to lay down this work that GOD was having me to do! While relaying the details to my prayer partner, I found that I unflinchingly declared in protest to the attack that, *"I refuse to come down from the work that I am doing to deal with this pettiness!"* You see, the tactic that the enemy used was supposed to make me intimidated, timid and afraid, and cause me to run in fear and become immobilized. But in the name of the Living GOD, I refused to come down to the level of the enemy and deal with the distraction that would have entangled me and kept me from completing the work that GOD had put in my hand!

As a focused and determined leader, Nehemiah gave me a revelation when he chose to stay on the wall and not come down to deal with pettiness, because the wall represents the high road. And that is the road you need to take when people try to bring you down to their level! Take the high road and refuse to descend!

Fight for Your Future!

Refusing to descend is also a part of fighting for your future.

Refusing to descend involves fighting your flesh and your carnal nature that desires to defend yourself and react to every person that attempts to come against you. Sometimes learning to fight involves learning how to be still and know that GOD is GOD. Allowing GOD to fight our battles as we learn to hold our peace is a combat strategy that seems easy in theory, however at times it can be difficult to practice. Although we say we trust GOD; when you are being provoked, or in the case of Nehemiah, falsely accused, there is oftentimes a desire to right the wrong and set the record straight.

I found myself in a season of people misrepresenting the truth, and I continuously tried to defend myself. I felt like I had to condemn every tongue that rose up against me. Consequently though, in this season, the Lord was trying to teach me to hold my peace and let Him fight my battles. On one occasion I did, and when GOD worked it all out, it was something to see. Not only did He give me the victory in that situation; but He also brought about reconciliation. When GOD mends conflict; it's going to have His fingerprint on it! – Love....

GOD was teaching me how to walk in lowliness, humility and gentleness. He was teaching me how to bear with others in love, and how to promote unity and keep the peace! This was the most humbling lesson because I could not even defend myself when I was in the right! Holding your peace means letting go of your ego!

Interestingly enough, through these times of testing I realized that when we do exercise the virtue of meekness in the face of persecution, we most resemble our Lord and Savior Jesus as we demonstrate a quiet strength!

The synonym for meekness is not weakness; but controlled strength! Yes, our greatest battle as we fight for our future may not always involve an actual opponent, but simply our own flesh as we learn to trust GOD and His deliverance. Learning to walk in the Spirit and respond in the Spirit, as opposed to reacting in the flesh, is all a part of fighting for our future. For we are fighting to grow in Christ and we are fighting to gain the maturity that we will need at the next level or dimension in GOD!

Fighting for your future may entail fighting the will to exert your will; in exchange for advancing the will of the Father. And GOD's will involves us learning to walk in the Spirit and operate in the fruit of the Spirit as found in Galatians 5:22-23. *"But the fruit of the Spirit is love, joy, peace, longsuffering, kindness, goodness, faithfulness, gentleness, self-control. Against such there is no law.*

Nehemiah refused to come down from his elevated position to deal with unfounded allegations, and because he did he accomplished a great work for the Lord; the walls were finished!

Mary rejected the opportunity to become intimidated or offended by the disciples, and as a result, her act of courage is memorialized in the Holy Bible, the most read book of all time!

GOD desires to use each and every one of us in similar fashion if we become determined to survive the pressure and the heat. We must, therefore, make up in our minds to endure the lengthy and trying process, be willing to persevere in the face of opposition while fighting for our future; and be willing to go through the refinement stage and to be ***polished to perfection...***

Chapter Four

Polished to Perfection

*"But may the God of all grace...after you have suffered a while, **perfect**, establish, strengthen and settle you."*
1 Peter 5:10

Anything that is created artistically involves various stages of production. And at least one of those stages involves a finishing off, a polishing if you will, that removes all of the residue of what it's been through in its formative process; and prepares it for its grand revealing to the world. *The same is true for diamonds...*

After surviving the pressure and high temperatures of the planet, pushing past all of the earth's elements, and being mined and collected by a manufacturer; diamonds must endure a finishing process prior to being presented to the consumer. This finishing process is needed because in their raw state, diamonds are unattractive. They are clouded, dull and rough. The light and splendor that is housed inside of a diamond is not apparent to the naked eye because the condition in which it has been created has seemingly masked its inerrant nature and value!

Part of the finishing process to unmask a diamond's magnificence is called "bruting." Bruting is when two diamonds are placed on an axle that rotates in opposite directions and allows the diamonds to brush against each other, thereby sanding away all of the dull finishes and releasing the brilliance.

Oftentimes as Christians, GOD places us in a "bruting" situation. He will allow us to share space and time with an individual that seemingly "rubs us the wrong way!" This person could be a boss, a co-worker, even a saint in the house of GOD who irks you tremendously and causes you to come out of character when you are interacting with them. They may illicit responses in you that seem out of the norm and they are such a challenge for you that they cause you to seek the very face of GOD for assistance. The interesting thing is that although it may be hard to believe, this person is really a diamond too! Just as they are rubbing you the wrong way, chances are, you are also rubbing them the wrong way too. And although this person may seem to bring out the worse in you; they are actually designed to bring out the best in you!

During this bruting, or sanding process, the very rough edges of your personality and character are removed. All of the dirt, the grime, and the residue of past hurt, offenses and trouble are sanded off, so that the dullness is gone, and GOD's Light can shine through you to bring Him the glory! Moreover, so that what emerges after the assignment is over is a vessel of honor fit for the Master's use!

A few years ago, GOD placed my diamond sandpaper in my life. Initially, this person and I got along very well. Then over time I began to notice that this person became very aggravating to me. They were very nitpicky and excessive, which drove me just about crazy and caused me to become out of character with them. I could not figure out what went wrong and how our relationship had taken this dreadful turn; until I saw a friend of my sandpaper and they asked me about how the two of us were doing. Before I could think these words sailed out of my mouth, *"They are bringing out the best in me!"* Those were clearly not the words I was searching for; but they were the words that the Lord filled my mouth with. And after they left my mouth they took a life of their own and brought revelation to me that this was the purpose of this person in my life; to smooth out my rough edges.

Interestingly enough, before GOD gave me this revelation I would not have considered this person as a diamond also. However, during my research I discovered that the only gem strong enough to cut and sand a diamond is another diamond; as there is no stronger gem on earth than a diamond. Thus, the person that is rubbing you the wrong way is probably in their own process with GOD also, and He is working on bringing out the best of them also.

The Bible declares in Psalm 42 that *"...deep calleth unto deep."* Therefore, although it may be hard to accept, that person that GOD designates in your life to be your sandpaper is a diamond; and GOD is also doing a work in them through you!

God desires to perfect us. Not to make us perfect, but to bring us into maturity!

Although polishing is necessary, it is not comfortable. A season of polishing is one that is marked with a series of tests that will reveal your true character and expose those quirks and issues in you that have not yet been perfected! The rough edges that are sanded off of your personality can be grueling and painful. It can also be humbling and gratifying if you submit to it. For if you are mature enough, you will recognize that GOD is doing a great work in you, and that He is not trying to harm you, but instead, bring you to an expected end. Begin to pray and ask God to allow you to see it from His perspective!

The Bible teaches us in the book of James how we should respond in this type of season. *"My brethren, count it all joy when you fall into various trials, knowing that the testing of your faith produces patience, but let patience have its perfect work, that you may be perfect and complete, lacking nothing. (James 1:1-4)*

GOD desires to perfect us! Not to make us perfect, but to bring us into maturity. The word "perfect" in the original Greek language means *"brought to its end; finished; wanting nothing necessary to completeness."* GOD desires that we walk in wholeness. Therefore, the polishing becomes necessary so that we will be prepared to handle the greater work that GOD has for us.

It's like when a wealthy parent passes away. Their child or heir may be too young to receive their inheritance, and so they put the inheritance into a trust fund until the child is eighteen or twenty-one years of age to receive it. They do not place a large amount of money or responsibility into their child's hands prematurely, because they know that the child is not responsible or mature enough to properly manage the inheritance. The same is true with us as GOD's children. He has to make sure that we come into a certain level of maturity to be able to handle the call or position that He has destined for us to inherit. The polishing test must be conducted to take away our rough, immature, and unpolished ways; preparing us for a greater level of responsibility in Christ!

The Bible declares in Psalm 37:23 that *"The steps of a good man are ordered by the Lord, And He delights in his way."* After I graduated from seminary in 2007, God began to order my steps into a series of career moves that landed me in positions and experiences where there were battles on just about every hand. During those years there was always either some type of injustice going on that I had to speak up about; or a difficult person that I really could not stomach, but had to learn to get along with them just the same. For years I questioned God as to whether I had heard Him correctly in the choices I had made and if I was still in the center of His will. It wasn't until the end of 2013 (the worst year of my life) that I began to ask God to show me this thing from His perspective. That is when I gained an understanding that I was exactly where He wanted me; on the Potter's wheel of perfecting!

God is sovereign, and He alone knows how to achieve the desired results in our lives to perfect us!

Jeremiah 18:2, 4 reads, *"Arise and go down to the potter's house...and the vessel that he made of clay was marred in the hand of the potter; so he made it again into another vessel, as it seemed good to the potter to make."* GOD is the Potter, and we are the clay. God desires to mold us and make us into a vessel that is good to Him. The word "good" in this verse means, *to make right, smooth, make straight.* Interestingly enough, that is what the polishing stage is about for diamonds; making them smooth, right and straight so that they are appealing for the consumer to purchase. God, our Potter, utilizes the potter's wheel to perfect us and make is appealing or good for Him to use! It is on the potter's wheel that he removes the bad attitude, He adjusts the judgmental attitude, He delivers us from the "woe is me" syndrome, and He destroys our invitation to a pity party. It is there that God refashions us and reshapes us into the vessel, the object, or the article that is "good" to Him to make; and that is able to carry His glory.

God is sovereign, and He alone knows how to achieve the desired results in our lives to perfect us. Oftentimes we receive a prophetic word spoken over our lives, and we are excited about it coming to pass. But rarely do we take the time to consider the fact that between the prophetic word being spoken, and the prophetic word being fulfilled, there is a process! And based on previous history, we can be assured that the process will be painful, and it will typically be prolonged!

No one probably knows this to be true better than Joseph. Joseph was the favored son of his father Jacob, because his mother Rachel was Jacob's favorite wife. The Bible tells us in Genesis 37:4 that *"...when his brothers saw that their father loved him more than all his brothers, they hated him and could not speak peaceably to him."* Joseph's favored position in the family, coupled with his dream of greatness and ruling over his brothers, positioned him to begin a journey of pain, betrayal and persecution. Joseph was excited when he dreamed in Genesis 37:7 and again in verse 9 that his brothers and parents would bow down to him and he would reign over them. He did not, however, expect that in order for the dream to be fulfilled, that he would have to endure such a grueling and heart wrenching polishing process!

Joseph was not positioned to reign in the kingdom as the second in command until he went through a finishing process of polishing. The series of unjust events in his life, coupled with his responses, were the necessary training needed to prepare him to lead a nation successfully in the time of crisis.

The Bible declares in Hebrews 12:11 that, *"Now no chastening for the present seemeth to be joyous, but grievous: nevertheless, afterward it yieldeth the peaceable fruit of righteousness unto them which are exercised thereby."*

While I'm sure that the trials and persecutions that Joseph endured were not enjoyable, they certainly developed him into the leader that God could use greatly. One whose light shined so bright, that he changed the course of a nation, and saved many people alive.

Polishing prepares...

Polishing produces...

Polishing promotes wholeness...

And while polishing may be painful, it is also purposeful!

While the finishing process is crucial and necessary to smooth away the rough surfaces of the diamond and release the ability of the diamond to display its internal light that is housed within; it is also vital in the life of a Christian as GOD works in us and through us to release His eternal light that is housed within us!

People of GOD, our lights shine the brightest when we are walking in what we have been put on this planet to do; when we are truly walking in and fulfilling **the destined Purpose for our lives...**

Chapter Five

Fulfilling your Purpose: Letting Your Brilliance Shine

*"Let your light so **shine** before men, that they may see your good works, and glorify your Father which is in heaven."*
Matthew 5:16

The light that is released in and through a diamond is what we refer to as its "brilliance.' A diamond's "brilliance" affects how much light is able to pass through the diamond. The ability to allow more light to pass through a diamond is what is called its "clarity," which affords the viewer a greater capacity to see and appreciate the depth of this beautiful gem in its entire splendor! Jesus instructed us in Matthew 5:16 to *"Let your light so shine before men, that they may see your good works, and glorify your Father which is in heaven."* If we are ever going to be able to bring God glory in our lives, then we are going to have to be able to submit to

God's process and polishing. For therein lies the way that God removes from within us those things that would hinder His Light from shining in and through us. Then, and only then, will we be able to take the Good News to a dark and dying world. For it is in the darkness, that His Light shines the brightest!

GOD's way of releasing the brilliance in us is not always orthodox, and certainly not the way that many of us would have chosen for ourselves; But as the Master Creator, GOD knows exactly what He is doing to achieve the best desired results and outcome; more clarity and brilliance!

The reason why we can be glory carriers, and show forth the brilliance of Christ's light, is because we have Christ in us, which is the hope of glory!

As I mentioned in the opening of this book, the title *"A Diamond in the Rough: Discovering the Brilliance in You"* was given to me by GOD to show the kindred process shared between the formation and finishing of a diamond; and the sanctification and maturing process of the believer.

Through this comparison, GOD wants us to ultimately know that every single believer has housed within us an internal and eternal Light that shines more brightly and with more clarity as we submit to His process, and allow ourselves to be changed more into His image.

The Bible declares in Colossians 1:26-27 that *"Even the mystery which hath been hid from ages and from generations, but now is made manifest to His saints: To whom GOD would make known what is the riches of the glory of this mystery among the Gentiles; which is Christ in you, the hope of glory."*

The reason why we can be glory carriers and show forth the brilliance of Christ's Light, is because we have Christ in us, which is the hope of glory! It is the Light of Christ that we are allowing to shine more freely. It is His shine that we are unveiling for the world to see. That is what we have been created to do; to bring God glory and worship with our lives! And because the riches of the glory of GOD have been deposited in us in the form of Christ Jesus; we can know with a surety that we are destined for greatness! This is why we can declare that we have a hope and a future!

It is the mystery of GOD that was concealed, but is now revealed in us and through us. Saints of GOD, we have JESUS, the Light of the world living inside of us. And as we grow in Christ and learn more about Him and His grace through our submission to His will, His brilliance begins to shine through us even more brightly. *"From glory to glory....."*

The purpose of a diamond is to shine brightly and release its brilliance so that others can appreciate its beauty. And GOD has created us to allow our lights to shine forth brightly as we discover our purpose in Him and walk in the fullness of His glory! The R&B singer Rihanna released a song called, *"Diamonds"* in 2012. I had already penned much of this book by then and I thought how prophetic her words were when she sang, *"Shine bright like a diamond."* God wants each of to shine bright with His glory as we live out what He has called each of us to do on this side of Heaven!

God never meant for our works or our light to be hidden under a bushel, or to be dimmed because of our fear of how others may interpret it!

The reason that most consumers purchase diamonds as the gem of choice for a wedding ring is that the diamond is durable, long-lasting, and emits a shine that resembles the glory that is upon their union. Diamonds are meant to show forth their brilliance and shine! That's why the young people call it "bling" because its shine is supposed to show forth marvelously and brilliantly!

As believers of the Lord Jesus Christ, it is GOD's design for us that we allow our lives and our service to Him to cast a brilliant light so that others may see; and it brings direct glory to Him as our Risen Savior and the One that called us into His service, and His marvelous light!

GOD never meant for our works or our lights to be hidden under a bushel or to be dimmed because of our fear of how others may interpret it! No, GOD means for our lights to shine forth out in the open where others can see it! *"No man, when he hath lighted a candle, putteth [it] in a secret place, neither under a bushel, but on a candlestick, that they which come in may see the light." (Luke 11:33)*

He will allow just enough hell in your life, to bring out the glory in your gifting!

I don't know about you, but many times I have allowed the whispers and judgments of other's thoughts and opinions to cause me to shrink back in fear and not let GOD use me the way that He designed to use me. I held back the way that I felt the prayer or the message was given to me by GOD, because of fear of rejection, or worse, fear of judgment. But GOD had to allow enough circumstances to bombard my life so that I became intolerant of and inoculated against caring what others thought about me. So much so, that I could move myself out of GOD's way and allow Him to bring Himself glory through me, by agreeing to let His brilliance shine in me.

The Bible declares in Romans 8:28, that, *"And we know that all things work together for good, to them that love the Lord, to them that are the called according to His purpose."* When you are called by GOD, He will allow everything to work together for your good...the storms, the valleys, the hardships, the persecution, and the lies being told on you; they all work together for your good. He will allow just enough hell in your life, to bring out the glory in your gifting!

Once you have gone through enough, you get to the point where it really doesn't matter anymore what anyone thinks about you, for you recognize that you were never designed to fit into a box that they created for you in the first place. Their box is too small! GOD has a substantially better plan for our lives than even you and I could comprehend!

When you are created to be used by GOD, you cannot compromise and shrink yourself to be fitted into man's categories or plans for you. Or even the ones you may have created for yourself. GOD's ways are not our ways, and His thoughts are higher than our thoughts! We can never imagine in our finite minds the full plan that GOD has for us; because His plans are always bigger, they are always better!

We have to resist the pulls of life and others to dumb down our anointing, or dim our light so that others can be comfortable with the category that they have prescribed for us. King Nebuchadnezzar wanted the Hebrew boys to be idol worshippers and compromise and worship him. But they were not called to bow down to idol worship; they were called instead to worship GOD by challenging the status quo, and to stand for GOD when all others had compromised!

GOD will not allow you to compromise the anointing that He has placed on your life just to go along to get along! My GOD! No... Narrow is the path to righteousness! Anyone can bow in order to have a reprieve from the persecution and the strife. But it takes a real warrior of GOD to stand up against wrong and answer the Nebuchadnezzar's in their lives back when they ask us, *"And who is the GOD who will deliver you from my hands?"* and tell them, *"O Nebuchadnezzar, we have no need to answer you in this matter. If that is the case, our GOD whom we serve is able to deliver us from the burning fiery furnace, and He will deliver us from your hand, O king. But if not, let it be known to you, O king, that we do not serve your GODs, nor will we worship the gold image which you have set up* (Daniel 3:15b-18).*"*

When you refuse to compromise, and you refuse to participate in idol worship, you are allowing GOD to shine forth His glory through you. GOD is looking for real worshippers, they that will worship HIM in spirit and in truth! He is not looking for timid placaters. No, He is looking for table turners and warriors for Christ that will allow GOD to use them to bring forth His will upon the earth!

Let your brilliance shine!

FULFILLING YOUR PURPOSE: LETTING YOUR BRILLIANCE SHINE

The reason diamonds are so expensive and valuable is because of the process that they have gone through; extreme, lengthy and trying. Most people can afford a cubic zirconium, but a diamond is a costly investment!

GOD has made a great investment in you and the anointing that is on your life. He has been there with you through thick and thin, the good times and the bad times. He has been bringing you along and refining your gift and increasing your anointing, all for His purposes! And now He is asking for a return, a dividend on His investment. He wants you to allow Him to use you, and for you to break forth as a Kingdom servant and a glory carrier! Let your brilliance shine!

If the truth be told, sometimes we are afraid to allow our brilliance to shine because we are fearful that the brightness may blind others. But in reality, if we allow our brilliance to shine, it will actually work to free others out of their own darkness, and give them permission to emancipate their own light for His glory!

My eldest son is a great father. When he is with his infant daughter JaHara, and she begins to cry, he simply looks at her and says, *"What's wrong? Don't worry!"* And then he goes on to state three very powerful words. He looks her in the eyes and states, *"I got you!"* Those words are very encouraging and comforting; especially spoken to a child from their father. Well, GOD knows what He is doing despite all of the time and trials that you have endured. And He is yet still looking you in your eyes and declaring, *"I got you!"* He knows how to position you and align you strategically so that your life, your anointing and your gifting, will be used to break the shackles off of the lives of others and facilitate a breakthrough in their situation!

Light dispels darkness. And who can argue in this day and time that darkness seems to be prevailing upon the earth. But I declare that if every one of us that has a call on our life in Christ would allow GOD's light to shine forth; we could dispel much of the crime, the poverty, the hatred, and the suffering of this world. GOD wants us. He wants you to break forth and allow Him to cultivate the gifts and the talents that are in you for His purposes. You were created to be a world changer; and GOD desires to change the world and advance His Kingdom through those of us that are yielded to Him. Let your brilliance shine!

GOD knew that He could trust you with the trouble, and then use you as His treasure!

All of the pressure, all of the heated situations, all of the dirt that you had to climb past, all of it has been allowed by GOD to fashion you, and to shape you into His glory carrier! He was there all along, watching over the process, holding the stop watch and timer on your pressure cooking situations.

Ford trucks have a slogan to inform the consumer of its greatest characteristics: strength and durability. They simply declare that they are "Built to Last." Just when you thought you couldn't take anymore; GOD allowed the test to go on a little bit longer in your life because He knew that you were built to last! He knew that you could handle more than you knew! He knew that you wouldn't crack under the pressure, but that you would use the pressure to polish you, and ultimately promote you! GOD knew what He put in you before the foundation of the world; a hope and a future that would not let your spirit die and that would cause you to achieve!

Yes, people talked about you and whispered, *"She/He must not be living right because of all of the hell that they are going through."* But GOD was saying all along, "I am building up a large enough audience, so that when I give you your breakthrough, it will be so great and so spectacular, it could only bring Me glory. They will declare that nobody else but GOD could have done it for you!"

I am talking to you woman of GOD, man of GOD, who have had a "hellafied" year, a challenging and tumultuous season, and who have wondered at times "GOD where are you?" GOD was simply preparing you for such a time as this; a time where He can use you to reach others; a time when He could use you to reach the nations, because you have the compassion and the heart because of what you have been through.

You are not about to go under, you are about to go over! You are about to see GOD's salvation and glory break forth as the noon day in your life! Your breaking was for the making of others!" GOD knew that He could trust you with the trouble, and then use you as His treasure! GOD knew that you would be dependable, and that you would not exit the process. He knew that greater was in you; even when you didn't know it yourself!

"It was never about punishment, only purpose! I took no joy in it being painful," saith the Lord, "but I knew it would be productive! I love you with an everlasting love. And now, my son, my daughter, I can raise you up and allow your light to shine, for "*Ye are the light of the world. A city that is set on a hill cannot be hid.*" (Matthew 5:14) "This is your time of revelation...your time of revealing. Let your brilliance come forth, let it shine forth, let it draw others to Me," saith the Lord! "Just as a diamond, I have allowed your process to birth out a precious, precious gem; one that is rare and has high value! You are valuable to Me and to My Kingdom here on earth. And I want to use you to bring glory to My name!"

Refuse to shrink back ever again! Refuse to dim or hide your light...let it shine!

GOD needs your brilliance to help illuminate the dark places of this world and to help spread the Gospel message, that Jesus is the Light of the World, and that He died to set men and women free!

All things truly do work together for those that love the Lord and are called according to His purpose! Every experience, every setback, every triumph, every disappointment, every success, every failure, every victory won, every battle lost, every line of pain and glory, GOD has been using it all to prepare you to share with the world the gifts and talents that He placed inside of you before the foundation of the world. *"Before I formed you in the womb, I knew you; before you were born I sanctified you; I ordained you a prophet to the nations." (Jeremiah 1:5)*

When your brilliance shines, it reveals your purpose!

Diamonds, although buried beneath the earth's surface are meant to be discovered and their beauty revealed and shared with others.

Left concealed in the womb of the earth, their brilliance and splendor would never be fully appreciated and admired. A diamond's purpose, one might argue, far exceeds adornment and accessorizing. As a symbol of strength, resilience and durability, diamonds are primarily used as the gem of choice for wedding rings to correlate its natural characteristics with the spiritual semblance of marriage. Positioned amidst a carefully selected setting that fits the gemstones shape perfectly, the diamond wedding ring is meant to demonstrate the covenantal strength and union that has been joined together by God. Therefore, the purpose of the diamond exceeds the aesthetic nature and points to a deeper exchange that has taken place between bride and groom.

The greatest existential question of humankind is, "What is the meaning of life?" Akin to that are the questions, "Why am I here?" And "What is my purpose?" A person can spend a lifetime trying to discover the meaning of these questions. Many embark upon a journey of self discovery in an attempt to find out why GOD created them and what is their intended contribution to this complexity called life. GOD declares in Jeremiah 29:11, *"For I know the thoughts and plans that I think toward you, says the Lord, thoughts and plans for welfare and peace and not for evil, to give you a hope in your final outcome." (Amplified)*

GOD knows the answer to these questions for each of us, and He is very clear about His thoughts and plans for our lives. Despite what we think, or the experiences we have had in our lives, GOD is adamant that His plans are for our welfare and peace. As Christians, our purpose (as explained in Romans 8:28) is birthed out of GOD's eternal plans and purposes. Therefore, our purpose is intricately woven into the overall purposes of GOD! And just as a diamond must be measured and fitted for its perfect setting; so have we been designed by GOD to fit into His overall plans for the Kingdom!

GOD placed that ministry, that business, that book, in you before you were even born; and He has been waiting for the appropriate time to release it and you upon the earth. What a wonderful, marvelous sight to see; the Potter's creation being released from the wheel to be shared with others.

Love is putting a demand on His gift!

You are a very precious jewel to GOD. You have great value and He wants to use you greatly! GOD desires for each and every one of us to reveal the inner illumination of His glory within us. As we mature in Christ, and as we learn to allow His presence and His light to illuminate us, others will be drawn to Him by our witness.

As you continue to trust GOD and His continued process in your life, you will, like Mary of Bethany in Chapter 3, be able to participate in divine events that will serve to have eternal implications. GOD will be able to use you to help change the trajectory of someone else's life for the good. As you avail yourself to the Father, He will enlarge your territory so that your light will shine in a greater measure and a broader span.

People of GOD, just as an oak tree is already existent within the acorn, and an apple tree in an apple seed, so is GOD's purpose and brilliance already housed in you! He placed His purpose in you before you were ever formed, and then He wrapped you in flesh and birthed you out of your mother's womb with greatness already concealed inside!

You will succeed! You must succeed! Because it was always in the will and mind of GOD for you to! Your calling lines up with GOD's Kingdom business for this hour, and it must be released! You are no longer stuck, but you are ready and being propelled by the Father to fulfill His will and purposes! Love is putting a demand

FULFILLING YOUR PURPOSE: LETTING YOUR BRILLIANCE SHINE

on His gift! Release and break forth your brilliance like the morning sun! It is time for others to experience the uniqueness that is you, and the glory of God that is upon your life!

IT IS TIME TO SHINE BRIGHT LIKE A DIAMOND...for you are no longer in the rough!

Our deepest fear is not that we are inadequate.

Our deepest fear is that we are powerful beyond measure. It is our light, not our darkness that most frightens us. We ask ourselves, "Who am I to be brilliant, gorgeous, talented, and fabulous?" Actually, who are you not to be? You are a child of GOD! Your playing small does not serve the world. There's nothing enlightened about shrinking so that other people won't feel insecure around you. We are all meant to shine, as children do. We were born to make manifest the glory of GOD that is within us. It's not just in some of us, it's in everyone, and as we let our own light shine, we unconsciously give others permission to do the same. As we are liberated from our own fear, our presence automatically liberates others.

Poem by Marianne Williamson
A Return to Love: Reflections on the Principles of A Course in Miracles (Ch 7, Sec 3, 1992)

About The Author

Catherine Griggs is a native of East Orange, New Jersey. She received her B.S. degree from Rutgers University, and her Master of Divinity from Drew Theological Seminary.

After working in the field of Social Work and Management for over 2 decades, Catherine transitioned into the Church, and presently serves as the Sr. Executive Assistant to the Bishop and Lead Pastor at Cathedral International Church in Perth Amboy, New Jersey, where she is also an Ordained Minister and Superintendent of Sunday School.

Catherine's greatest role to date is that of mother to her two sons John and Malcolm, Glam Ma to JaHara and Laila, and wife to John Sr.

To have the author speak at your conference or event you can contact her at:

The Reverend Catherine Griggs
Diamond Ministries
diamond.ministries@yahoo.com
Facebook: Diamond Ministries

Order Information

You can inquire about ordering additional books by sending email to: diamond.ministries@yahoo.com

You can order additional copies of *A Diamond In The Rough* by going to the publisher's website at:

www.DPC-Books.com

Also available at Amazon.com
In Paperback and Kindle

www.ingramcontent.com/pod-product-compliance
Lightning Source LLC
Chambersburg PA
CBHW071147090426
42736CB00012B/2259